Living in a Community

by Barbara M. Linde

Table of Contents

Introduction

People live in **communities**. Read about different communities.

▲ People live in this community.

city

communities

country

goods

neighbors

services

suburb

work

See the Glossary
on page 22.

3

What Is a Community?

A community is a place. People live in a community. People live near each other. People are **neighbors**.

▲ Neighbors live near each other.

A community is a place. People **work** in a community.

It's a Fact
People have fun in communities also.

▲ This bus driver works in a community.

▲ People have fun at a park.

A community is a place. A community has stores. Stores have **goods**. People buy the goods.

▲ Clothes are goods.

▲ Groceries are goods.

A community is a place. A community has **services**.

▲ Schools are services.

▲ Libraries are services.

7

What Is an Urban Community?

An urban community is a **city**. Many people live in a city.

▲ Many people live in this city.

A city has many homes. The homes are close together.

sOlve This

Six Largest Cities in the United States

City	Population*
New York	8,008,278
Los Angeles	3,694,820
Chicago	2,896,016
Houston	1,953,631
Philadelphia	1,517,550
Phoenix	1,321,045

*2000 census

Many people live in Phoenix. More people live in New York. How many more people live in New York?

Answer: 6,687,233

▲ Homes are close together in this city.

Many people work in a city. Some people work in offices.

▲ People work in this office.

Some people work in stores.

▲ People work in this store.

A city has many stores. Stores sell goods.

▲ **This store sells many goods.**

A city has many services. A city has police. A city has firefighters. A city has hospitals.

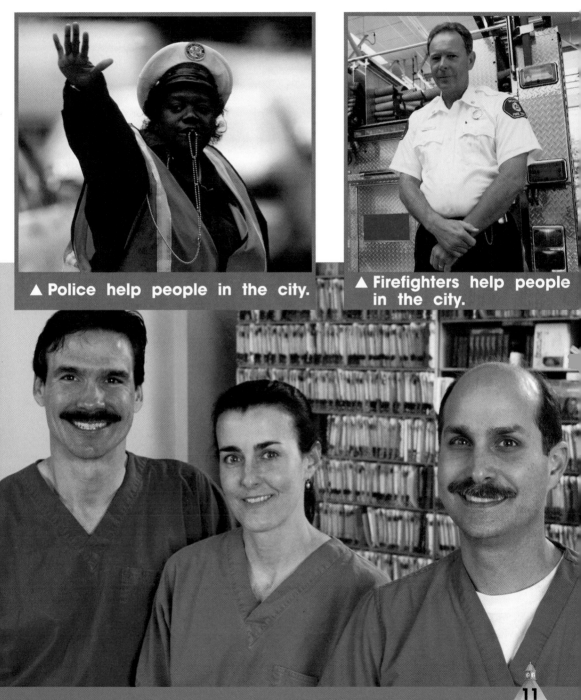

▲ Police help people in the city.

▲ Firefighters help people in the city.

▲ Doctors help people in a city hospital.

What Is a Suburban Community?

A suburban community is a **suburb**. Many people live in a suburb. A suburb has many homes.

▲ People live in houses.

▲ A suburb is near a city. Streets go to the city.

▲ A suburb has many people.

▲ People live in apartments.

Many people work in a suburb. Some people work in offices.

▲ People work in this office buildin

Some people work in stores.

▲ People work in this store.

A suburb has shopping malls. There are many stores in shopping malls.

▲ People shop in shopping malls.

▲ This store has pets.

A suburb has many services. A suburb has police. A suburb has hospitals. A suburb has schools.

▲ Police help people in this suburb.

Figure It Out

What services do you and your family use?

▲ This hospital is in a suburb.

▲ Students in this suburb go to school.

What Is a Rural Community?

A rural community is in the **country**. A rural community has few people. A rural community has few homes.

▲ A rural community is smaller than a city.

Then & Now

Los Angeles was a rural community.

Now Los Angeles is a large city.

People work in a rural community. Some people work in stores. Some people work on farms. Some people work on ranches.

▲ People work in this store.

▲ People work on this farm.

▲ People work on this ranch.

A rural community has few stores.

BOOT SHOP
SHOE REPAIR

ANTIQUES

ANTIQUES
BY BILLIE

HALE COUNTY TEACHERS
FEDERAL CREDIT UNION

MO

▲ **This rural community has stores.**

A rural community has services. A rural community has schools.

▲ Students ride buses to this school.

A rural community has doctors.

▲ This doctor works in a rural community.

People live and work in communities. Communities have stores. Communities have services.

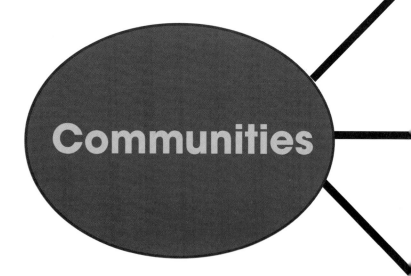

Communities

Think *About It*

1. What is a community?

2. What kind of community do you live in? Tell about it.

Urban Community

a city
many people
many homes
people work
stores
services

Suburban Community

a suburb
near a city
many people
many homes
people work
services

Rural Community

in the country
smaller than a city
few people
few homes
people work
services

city a very large community

*Houston is a **city**.*

communities places where people live and work

*People live in and work in **communities**.*

country a large area that is not in a city

*A rural community is in the **country**.*

goods things people buy

*Groceries are **goods**.*

neighbors people who live near each other

Neighbors live in a community.

services things people need

Libraries are services.

suburb a community near a city

A suburb has many homes.

work to do a job

People work in communities.

Index